9/97

4/00

5x (5/03) 10/10

S0-CBZ-334

CR

SAN DIEGO PUBLIC LIBRARY
CHILDREN'S ROOM

The World of Work

Choosing a Career in
Law Enforcement

If you are looking for an exciting, rewarding, and steady job, the field of law enforcement might be for you.

The World of Work

Choosing a Career in Law Enforcement

Claudine G. Wirths

SAN DIEGO PUBLIC LIBRARY
CHILDREN'S ROOM

3 1336 04501 3209

THE ROSEN PUBLISHING GROUP, INC.
NEW YORK

Published in 1997 by The Rosen Publishing Group, Inc.
29 East 21st Street, New York, NY 10010

Copyright 1997 by The Rosen Publishing Group, Inc.

All rights reserved. No part of this book may be reproduced in any form without permission in writing from the publisher, except by a reviewer.

First Edition

Library of Congress Cataloging-in-Publication Data

Wirths, Claudine G.
    Choosing a career in law enforcement / Claudine G. Wirths.
        p.   cm.— (The World of work)
    Includes bibliographical references and index.
    Summary: Offers an overview of careers in law enforcement, including police officer, security guard, and private investigator.
    ISBN 0-8239-2274-X
    1. Law enforcement—Vocational guidance—United States—Juvenile literature.   2. Police—Vocational guidance—United States—Juvenile literature.   [1. Law enforcement—Vocational guidance.   2. Police—Vocational guidance.   3. Vocational guidance.   4. Occupations.]
    I. Title.   II. Series: World of work (New York, N. Y.)
    HV7922.W55   1997
    363.2′3′02373—dc20   96-17626
                                                                      CIP
                                                                       AC

Manufactured in the United States of America

Contents

Introduction

What do you imagine when you think of a career in law enforcement? Do you see yourself racing down an alley, firing at a mugger? Or racing through the streets in a souped-up squad car? You see these kinds of police jobs on television, but they are only a small part of the real world of law enforcement.

The real world of law enforcement includes dozens of jobs besides the police officer on the street. They include night watchman, border patrol officer, building guard, and park ranger. All these jobs are filled by everyday people like you, not by television stars.

Law-enforcement work is important because laws help us live together in peace and safety. Sadly, not everyone cares about peace and safety. Someone has to make sure that the laws are obeyed. Law enforcers are the people who do that. They are needed.

Law-enforcement workers enforce laws.

Some people, such as patrol officers, patrol neighborhoods in cars or on foot. They chase speeders. They arrest people who commit crimes. They defend people in trouble. They often work in the face of danger.

Other workers support those officers. They do such things as study fingerprints, write reports, and keep records. They rarely face danger, but their work is important to everyone.

Still others have jobs that remind us to obey laws. Just by being seen, security guards in buildings and night watchmen remind us to do the right thing. These workers are rarely in danger, but they have to be prepared for it.

Is Law Enforcement for You?

Only you can answer that question. Many people in law-enforcement jobs like their work. It is satisfying because it gives them action, steady work, the ability to help others, and a close community.

Law enforcement is often exciting. Some jobs are especially well suited for people who like to be in on the action.

Many government jobs in law enforcement are long-term. They often have good retirement and health plans.

Most people in law enforcement have two things in common. They respect the law, and they respect other people.

Law-enforcement workers protect people, their homes, and their property.

Law-enforcement people tend to stick together. When trouble comes, they often protect each other and care for each other's families.

Would You Be Good at Law Enforcement?

You may be wondering if you are the right kind of person to be in law enforcement. A good law-enforcement person has several qualities.

He respects the laws and respects other people. Laws are the same for everyone. Race, sex, or age do not matter. A good worker would not take a bribe—money, or something else of value—to let someone, even a friend, break the law. A good law-enforcement person would not hurt someone unless he thought it was necessary in the line of duty.

She obeys the law. Since she enforces the law, she must also obey it.

He follows orders. Most law-enforcement groups are run like the military. Workers often wear uniforms. They hold ranks, which means that each person has a rank, or title. Certain titles, like "police chief," have more power than others, like "patrol officer." They are given orders. At times such an order may put them in great danger.

She is trustworthy. Law enforcers are often asked to guard drugs, cars, or large sums of money. They are trusted not to steal, not even small things like a CD or a few dollars.

He can keep a secret. Most law-enforcement jobs require the workers to keep secrets. Workers may know about a store's security system, the facts of a case, or police plans, but they must discuss it only with other law enforcers. They must never tell friends or family.

If you possess these qualities, then a career in law enforcement may be ideal for you.

Finding a Job in Law Enforcement

You'll find jobs in law enforcement in four main places. Local governments, state governments, the federal government, and private companies each need law enforcers.

Local government agencies hire people for jobs with the county or city. Examples are sheriff's deputies, city police, county patrols, and jailers.

State governments hire workers for the state to serve as state patrol officers, corrections officers, natural resources police, and crime lab workers, for example.

The United States government hires workers for the border patrol, U.S. Customs, the Coast Guard, and the National Park System.

Private companies hire people to work as mall security, bodyguards, private investigators, and armored-car drivers.

Each of these kinds of jobs will be discussed at greater length in the following chapters.

What Else Do You Need to Know?

You need to know five things before you plan a life in law enforcement:

- You must be a citizen of the United States for any government job.
- You can get a job even if you do not finish high school—but you will be paid more if you have a high school diploma.
- You need to go to college for a year or more for the best-paid jobs.
- You will receive training after you are hired. This training may be as little as a day or two or as much as three months.
- You can work full-time or part-time in law enforcement.

In this book you'll read the stories of people who work in the field of law enforcement. What they have to say can help you decide if one of these jobs is the right career for you.

Questions to Ask Yourself

It takes certain qualities to be a successful law-enforcement officer. 1) What are those qualities? 2) Do you have some or all of those qualities? If so, which ones?

Police officers work for the municipal or city government.

Working for Municipal or County Government 1

My name is Terry, and I live in a middle-sized city in Maryland. From the time I was a little kid I wanted to be a police officer. In high school I did not study hard at first. Then my dad told me that if I wanted to be a police officer I would have to finish high school. So I tried harder and finally graduated.

In my city you can join the police force by becoming a police cadet as soon as you get out of high school. That's what I decided to do. To be a regular officer on the police force you have to be twenty-one, but I didn't want to wait till then.

I first went to the municipal (city) personnel office. That's where people are hired. I filled out a lot of papers. Then I scheduled an appointment for a physical and some written exams.

The day of the exams, they really checked me out. They do that whether you are going to be a cadet or an officer. I had to pass a medical *exam. That didn't worry me. I had passed a physical to play high school sports. I knew I was okay for police height and weight requirements too. A bunch of other physical tests showed how well I could see, and how strong and quick I was. I also had to take some written tests.*

While I was taking these tests, they checked my record to find out if I had ever been in trouble with the police. That scared me a little, because when I was ten I was caught shoplifting some candy. The officer told me that since I hadn't done anything worse as I got older, that was okay. But if I had been arrested for breaking into someone's house when I was sixteen, they would have rejected my application.

They tested me for drugs, and I was clean. If I had had any traces of drug use in my body, I would have failed. They gave me a lie detector test and asked me if I had ever used drugs or alcohol. I said I hadn't used drugs, but I had drunk some beer on a few weekends. They told me since I was telling the truth, I would pass. But they said I would have to cut out any drinking until I was of legal age, twenty-one. They said they would check me every once in a while.

The police department also needed reference letters. I asked my school counselor, my minister, and some other people to write reference letters for me. They were asked to say whether I could be trusted and whether I stayed calm even when others got upset.

I also had to have a driver's license with no points on it, meaning that I had not been caught breaking any traffic laws.

A few weeks later I received a letter that said I was in!

As a police cadet I didn't make much money, but I did wear a uniform. The first thing they did was to send me back to school. Three mornings a week I went to the police academy with other cadets. We learned about the laws in our city. As a cadet, I couldn't make arrests. Instead I washed patrol cars, made lists of what officers brought in after arrests, and even helped on an undercover operation, or sting.

A sting is an undercover operation, so I wasn't in uniform. I was sent into a store to buy wine. Two officers outside the store watched, but they stood where the cashier couldn't see them. The clerk sold me wine and didn't ask me for an ID, so he was arrested. He gave me a really dirty look and called me all kinds of *names. But having people mad at you is a fact of life in police work.*

When I turned twenty-one, I was sworn in as a police officer. At first I was on probation. Probation means that I had one year to prove I was fit to be a police officer. I had to go to the police academy for a month. That is where I really learned about guns, how to do traffic work, and lots more. We had to write reports and learn how to present cases in court.

After that, I went to work with an older officer. What he taught me about policing went beyond what was covered in the course work. Sometimes we were in a patrol car. Other times we walked or bicycled around the streets. We were responsible for an area of our town and tried to get to know the people on our beat.

We did lots of different jobs. We directed traffic, answered calls, and helped at car accidents. Sometimes we staked out places where we thought a crime would happen. We chased speeders and ticketed people who ran stop signs. Much of the time the work was just plain boring. Other times it was as action packed as it is on television.

That first year seemed to last a long, long time. There were officers I didn't like very much at first. But I also knew my life might

The thought of high-speed chases and catching people who have broken the law is exciting to many people.

depend on them some day, so I learned to get along with them.

What don't I like about police work? I don't like the idea that I might have to kill someone some day. I don't like arresting people I know. That happens sometimes. I also don't like having my hair cut this short, but my dad does. I wish I made more money, but it's steady work. I'm not likely to be laid off. And after a couple of years I can make more money, if I pass the tests and move up in rank.

What do I like? I like night-shift work. I like working when everyone else is asleep. I'm glad that people sleep safer because of me. Being

As a police officer, you may have to do some jobs that you don't like, such as arresting someone you know.

outdoors a lot is great too. So is working with a partner. And I like the exciting times when the station is alive with everyone working on a big case. I guess I like being where the action is!

Terry's story tells you a lot about the career of a police officer in most places. But police work will not be exactly the same where you live. Some places do not have a program for *cadets*, people who are in long-term training to become police officers. Some hire *police officers* as young as age nineteen. Small towns pay less than big cities. Some cities want new employees to have at least one year of college. However, all do send their future officers to a *police academy* for training. If you are interested, find out more about the department in the town or city where you live.

Other Areas of Local Law Enforcement

Deputy sheriffs work for the county instead of the city. Sometimes they serve as the police for an entire rural county. They do some arrests and patrolling. But sheriff's deputies also carry important county papers to people's homes. They police the courthouse and take prisoners to court. Deputy sheriffs have to pass the same tests as police officers.

Jailers work at a city or county jail. They learn their work on the job. Most of the people in jail have committed lesser crimes and are there for only a short time. Jailers check prisoners in and take care of their clothes and money. They keep records on the prisoners. They give them food, sheets, towels, and clothes. The more years a jailer works, the higher the pay.

Court deputies keep order in county courthouses. They have other jobs as well. They stand by to be sure the jury is chosen correctly. They see to it that the jurors have food and are protected from anyone talking to them. If the jury has to stay overnight, court deputies may guard the jury in a hotel. They may also work with the person who maintains the court's records, the court clerk. They check to be sure trials are held in the right rooms. They see to it that the people are there when they're needed. They go to police classes and receive on-the-job training.

Dispatchers answer the emergency phones. They send help when needed. Dispatchers must be good at handling many jobs at one time. Sometimes they get five or six calls at once and have to decide how to handle all of them. They must pass written tests, speak clearly, keep cool in a crisis, and know how to use a computer. The training may be on the job or in a special program.

Other Local Government Jobs

If a county has a county police system as well as a sheriff, *county police* handle most of the crime work and traffic control.

Transportation guards watch television monitors to check for problems on elevators or on platforms of subway systems.

Animal control officers pick up stray animals and enforce animal laws.

Port wardens enforce laws on boats docking at a port.

Questions to Ask Yourself

Many law enforcement positions are available in the municipal or county government.
1) What are some of those jobs? 2) Does your area offer a police cadet program? 3) How can you contact the police recruiting officer in your town?

Working for the State Government

2

My name is Donnell, and I'm a guard at a state prison. My real title is "corrections officer." I didn't intend to work here when I got out of high school. Then I lost my job at the supermarket. I was about to turn twenty-one, so I applied at the state personnel office for a job at the prison. I passed a short test that showed I could read and follow directions. The physical was tough. I wished I had worked out more before I took it, but I passed.

I soon found out that this is no easy job. I went to school for three months right in the prison. We learned how to talk to prisoners, how to care for guns—and how to shoot to kill. I learned how to defend myself if someone jumps me. I also learned how to hold a prisoner who is violent. We were even trained to handle riots.

At first I was scared. Some of the people in my prison are murderers and muggers. But I found that most of them are just your average guy who caused trouble.

I work an eight-hour day, but I have to be ready to work whenever they need me. Last year I had to work New Year's Eve although it wasn't my shift.

The starting pay isn't bad. I'll be a sergeant next year if I pass the tests. I will make a good deal more money and even live on the prison grounds. The state will provide a house and health care for me and my family.

Don't go into this job unless you are sure of your interest. The work requires lots of patience. You also need to be smart and strong. I have to stay calm if someone murders someone in my area. I have to help inmates understand legal work. I listen to them when someone in their family dies. I provide their basic needs— toothpaste, soap, toilet paper. I have to keep my temper, not lash out at the ones who yell at me. At the same time, I must be ready at any second to defend my life. This is not a job for someone who scares easily. But you help people who really need help. I'm glad I took the job.

Pay scales vary in different prisons, but the training, working conditions, and duties are much the same in both state and federal prisons. If you like a tough job, check out the prison nearest you.

Other State Jobs in Law Enforcement

There are a number of other state-funded jobs in law enforcement that you might like. You can inquire at the state personnel office about them. Most of these jobs require at least a high school diploma.

State patrol officers have much the same duties as city police, but they may have to work in various parts of the state. The state is usually divided into districts called barracks. An officer may be sent to work at any of the barracks.

Many places have a cadet program. *Cadets* can enter right out of high school if they pass physical and psychological tests. They receive on-the-job training. They spend their time doing jobs like weighing trucks to make sure the truck's weight doesn't exceed the regulations. When cadets turn twenty-one, they are hired as full-time officers unless they have failed as cadets. As full-time patrol officers they go to school for several weeks to learn the laws of the state and how to handle guns and shoot.

The job of the state patrol is to enforce

Highway patrol officers enforce the laws governing road travel.

state laws. They may protect the governor and other state officials. They usually work with rangers to enforce laws in parks and forests. They also answer calls for help and go to crime scenes. They control traffic on state and interstate roads and help at accidents. They must be good at writing reports and testifying, or giving oral reports, in court.

They need to stay physically fit. The work is tiring, and officers may have to drive for hours. An officer who passes tests can be promoted and make more money.

Highway patrols handle only traffic in most states. They often have limited police powers. Their job is to enforce speed laws, handle accidents, and help motorists in trouble. They pass tests similar to the state patrol to get their jobs.

Natural resources police are the people who police outdoor areas. They must meet the same age and educational requirements as do state patrol officers. They may also have to learn to ride a horse, pilot a boat, or drive a snowmobile. They check on hunting, fishing, and boating licenses. They work in all types of weather. They have to be able to lift heavy objects, climb cliffs, run after suspects, and crawl through caves or walk across deserts.

Fingerprint classifiers are careful, detail-oriented people.

They often face physical danger. They may work alone and must be ready to work whenever they are needed. This is a job for people who like the outdoors and understand those who enjoy outdoor sports. They work closely with park and forest rangers.

Crime lab technicians help solve crimes by studying the evidence from a crime scene. Some match bullets to guns. Some check handwriting on checks. Some go to the scene of a wreck and study the cars and tire tracks. Technicians must be good with cameras and lab equipment. They often testify in court and must be able to write a good report and speak

27

well in public. This is a good job for someone who likes science and is neat and careful. It usually requires at least one or two years of college.

Fingerprint classifiers work with fingerprints. Are you good at details? Do you like keeping records? Do you make few errors in your work? Can you work with a computer? Large state crime labs hire people who do nothing but classify and compare fingerprints all day. There are also jobs in the federal government for fingerprint experts. It is slow work. It is also stressful. A life may hang on your finding the right fingerprint. If this field interests you, you need to take courses in criminal justice and photography.

Lifeguards often work only part-time, but in some states the job is full-time. It also may be a local government job. Lifeguards may work at an indoor pool in a state park or outside at a pool or lake or beach. The lifeguard enforces rules and protects public property. When a state owns a section of beach, the lifeguard may remind people about the laws that deal with using the beach. Lifeguards must have good health and pass first-aid and lifesaving tests.

Other Job Prospects in Your State

Fire wardens watch for forest fires, enforce fire laws, and help put fires out.

Park rangers protect visitors and enforce state laws in parks.

Bailiffs keep order in courtrooms.

Look around your state and you will find there are jobs in courthouses, parks, and forests. But don't forget to look at United States government jobs too.

Questions to Ask Yourself

There are several law enforcement opportunities within the state government for people who don't want to work on patrol. 1) What are those types of jobs? 2) Which type of job, if any, interests you? 3) What about that kind of job interests you?

Park rangers are law enforcement officers in the national parks.

United States Government

3

My badge reads S. Grissom. The S stands for Sandra, but everyone calls me Sandy. As a park ranger, I'm a law enforcement officer in a national park. I chose the work because I like being outside—rain or shine, hot or cold. Many parks need law-enforcement people these days. But the National Park Service wants you to be good at something besides law enforcement. That can be history, wildflowers, rescue work, or something else. I got my job because I went to a two-year college and know a lot about fish. Also, I worked at the park every summer, and that helped me get the job.

To be a ranger I had to be twenty-one, and pass oral and written tests and a medical exam. Once hired, I went to a training program to learn park rules and my duties. Then they sent me to Federal Law Enforcement Training School (FLETC) for six weeks.

School work was easier for the rangers who had four years of college, but I worked hard and passed. We learned criminal, civil, and traffic laws as well as park and forest laws. We learned to use and care for guns. We wrote reports and spoke in front of the group. We even learned to fight forest fires.

Most park visitors obey the laws, but not all of them. Once we arrested a man who had set fire to a campground. Some drug dealers hid out in our forest too, and I helped capture them. In some parks, the rangers help the local police. In my park we're the only police. We do everything.

Mostly I give talks to school kids about the fish in our lake. At those times, I don't wear a gun. But when I'm on patrol I wear a bullet-proof vest and carry a gun. I don't like wearing body armor because it's heavy and not made for women, but I wear it to be safe.

To be good at a job like mine, you have to stay alert. You must make quick decisions. You have to be able to shift quickly from talking about wildflowers to looking for an illegal hunter.

Every year I go to training programs for two or three days. We learn about changes in the laws and new rules for the parks and forests. Even after ten years I wouldn't trade my job for any other. I know that my work helps keep our *park safe for everyone. And I help save the forests and parks.*

Most park and forest rangers are expected to be law-enforcement officers these days. Check with the park and forest department in your state as well as the National Park Service for jobs. In these jobs you may work almost alone or you may be in a park with thousands of visitors. You may be sent to other parks as you move up. You must be good at planning and carrying out your work. At the same time, you must be able to get along well with people.

Other Federal Law-Enforcement Jobs

The following federal government jobs mostly require at least a high school diploma.

Building guards don't need experience to begin work. However, a veteran of the armed forces, such as the Army, Navy, Air Force, or Marines, stands the best chance to be hired. Guards are sent to school to learn to handle guns. They learn other duties on the job. Some guards sit or stand at the entrances of government buildings. They check photo badges to be sure the person has a right to be there. They check that no one is carrying guns or bombs in a package. Other guards patrol the building. They answer questions and give directions to people. Night-shift guards walk through the building to be sure doors are locked, files closed, and windows shut. They also watch for fires and people who should not be in the building. Many guards are on their feet all the time, which can be very tiring. The work is steady. There is not much chance to advance, but you receive good health care, vacations, and a retirement plan.

Border patrol officers often work alone and must make good decisions on their own. This isn't the job for anyone who doesn't want to work hard and study hard. To be in the border patrol you must pass tough physical, written, and oral tests. Once hired, you are sent to FLETC for eighteen weeks to learn law enforcement and Spanish. When you graduate you receive twenty-four weeks of on-the-job training.

Officers check roads, trains, planes, and boats to find people who entered the country illegally. Because some of these people are dangerous, officers often risk their lives.

Border patrol work is hard on family life. The officers are often away from home for long periods of time. They may be sent

Customs workers make sure that illegal items, such as drugs or weapons, don't enter or leave the country.

anywhere from the border with Canada to the border with Mexico or anywhere along either coast. Families may have to move many times. But the job has the usual good benefits for those who work for the U.S. government.

Customs workers are hired to work at a place of entry into the United States. That could be an airport, a dock, or a border crossing. They carry out the laws about what may leave the country and what may come in. They check for drugs or other illegal things. They check for stolen cars or other goods that someone might try to send out. They also collect both duty and taxes from tourists for some items bought in other countries.

You need to be twenty-one to join, and it helps if you know at least two languages. It helps also to know a lot about some field such as jewels or clothing. This is shift work, which means that you work in eight-hour shifts. The shifts can be during the day, evening, or night. It can be dangerous.

If you like the ocean and boats, consider the *Coast Guard*, a military service that enforces the laws of the sea and rescues people in danger out at sea. The Coast Guard requires at least a high school education. To be hired, you must be at least seventeen, pass the physical, and score at least 40 percent on the Armed Services Vocational Aptitude Battery (ASVAB), a test everyone takes to join the armed services. If accepted, you are sent to basic training for eight weeks. Then you are sent to a Coast Guard unit. At that unit you will train for an additional twelve to twenty-four weeks to learn a skill, such as boating or health care. After that you will be assigned to a unit that needs your skills. You can retire after twenty years with a good retirement package.

Postal police officers must be twenty-one

Joining the armed services is one way to enter the field of law enforcement.

and physically fit. They need to have good
hearing and good eyesight. They must be able
to read and write well and get along with
people. To get the job, you must take a written
test.

Many people think the federal government
runs the post office. It does not. The post
office is privately run, but it has many of the
federal government job benefits. Postal police
officers guard post offices, both inside and
outside. They may work at the loading docks
where postal trucks park. They may sit inside
the door and check badges of people who go
into the mailroom. Check the bulletin board at
your local post office for a list of openings.

Other U.S. Government Jobs

Immigration guards guard immigrants until they are admitted to the United States or sent back to their own country.

The *U.S. Army* and *U.S. Navy* train people to be *military police.* Many law-enforcement jobs give preference to veterans. As a result, being in any of the services is a good way to start a career in law enforcement.

If you don't like working for a government agency, you will find that many private businesses hire law-enforcement people. If you have a police record and cannot work for the government, consider working for a private business. If you have changed your ways and proved your dependability, some companies will hire you. Read on to find out what jobs are out there.

Questions to Ask Yourself

Your choices for a career within the federal government are varied. 1) If you like nature, what type of job would appeal to you? 2) What jobs would be good for someone who enjoys traveling? 3) Which job, if any, appeals to you? Why?

Working for a Private Company

4

My name is Cora. I work as a security guard at a mall. When I finished high school, I went to work as a building guard for a big company. At that particular job I sat at a desk all day long and checked people in and out. I found it boring.

After two years I applied for this job at the mall. I like it because I get to move around. I have regular hours and regular pay. I wear a uniform and carry a small two-way radio so I can quickly go where I am needed. But I don't carry a gun or a club. I don't even have a bullet-proof vest. I am supposed to talk people out of causing trouble.

When I signed up I was given only two days of on-the-job training. A police officer came in and told us what we could do and what we could not do. He said we cannot make arrests; we can only detain people. That means we can only tell people to stop what they are doing or ask them to leave the mall. He told us to call the police if we had to handle fights or other big problems.

As I walk around the mall I watch for people who might be sick or who seem to need help. I check to be sure restrooms are clean and no one is causing a problem in them. I check to be sure fire doors are unlocked during the day.

I don't look for shoplifters. If a store in the mall catches a shoplifter, they may call me. I watch them check out the person. If the store calls the police, I go to court to tell what I saw.

We keep lists of people who have been ordered not to come into the mall. If someone comes in who is not supposed to be there, I ask them to leave. I have to spot these people before they make trouble.

The night guard makes sure that everyone is out when the mall closes. He checks to be sure doors and windows are locked and that the parking lots are secure.

Sometimes even this job is slow. Nothing happens for days at a time. Then something big happens, and I help the police catch someone. I like feeling that I have helped.

The best thing about the job is all the people I meet—but that's also the worst thing about it. Sometimes I meet people who try to cause me trouble. Because I am a petite African-

American woman, some people think they can bully me. But I don't let them. I take the attitude that I do my job. When they see I mean business, they go along with me.

When I started, I was paid just a little better than minimum wage. Now that I have been here a couple of years, I make more money. But there is not much higher I can go in this job. I'll either have to do some other work at the mall or join a police force.

Most malls hire *security guards* and *night guards*. They want people who are clean, neat, and attentive. Workers must be on time. Night workers are more likely to face danger.

The most important part of the job is dealing with the public. The mall wants workers who get along with people. They want workers who help the public first and enforce rules second. There are no particular educational requirements for security guards, although a high school diploma usually helps.

Some large malls in high-crime areas do not hire security guards like Cora. They hire off-duty police officers.

Other Private Jobs

Store security guards are hired by many large

Security guards must always be alert and aware of what's going on around them.

stores, both in the malls and out. The guards wear everyday clothes and walk around the store. They look for shoplifters and watch clerks to be sure they don't steal.

Some stores have automatic alarms that sound when someone tries to take something out of the store without paying for it. The store security guard stops the person and asks to see the packages. They have to do this politely because the person may have paid, but the clerk forgot to remove the alarm tag.

Private investigators (PIs), or private eyes, are hired by people to investigate a situation.

They may look for someone who has run away. They may try to discover whether someone is stealing from his boss. They may photograph a man who is cheating on his wife.

Most states require PIs to have no police record and to take a course if they are going to carry a gun.

Some agencies send new hires out with another PI to be trained. The best agencies want workers who have gone to a school for private investigators. Often these schools also find jobs for students who graduate. There is a high dropout rate from the schools because many people find they do not like the work.

Be sure that the company you want to work for has a state license. You could get into trouble with the law if your company does not have one.

A good PI must be curious about everything, write well, and have a good memory. If you do well at the work, you can make a very good salary after a few years. People start at a little over minimum wage.

Night watch workers guard businesses at night. Most business owners hire someone who has already had a job as a security guard. The person may have to work with a guard dog. This is a job for someone who can stay awake all night and work alone. It may be dangerous. No training is needed unless the job requires that you carry a gun.

Airport security personnel check bags and passengers before passengers board planes. They are hired by the company that runs the airport. They wear uniforms and must be polite. They try to spot people who look guilty or afraid. Their job is to find anyone carrying a gun, knife, or bomb. A good person for this job is one who has a sixth sense about people and can spot a person who plans to cause trouble. Workers are taught to use metal detectors and X-ray machines and told what to look for in bags. Workers cannot let people hurry them or distract them.

Armored car drivers and guards are men and women who transport money to and from banks. They are hired by a security company or by a bank. Armored car drivers and guards carry weapons and are trained to handle them. They rarely face danger, but when they do, it is major danger, usually someone trying to steal the money. This is a job for a person who can stay alert even when nothing much is happening—which is most of the time.

Security agency workers are hired by some companies part time to do small security jobs.

Airport security personnel are responsible for making sure no weapons or illegal items are brought onto airplanes.

To do this you need to be adaptable. In one job you might control traffic or the crowd at a music concert. In another job you might give directions to a meeting room. You might have to guard gifts at a wedding reception.

Starting workers receive minimum wage. Many of these companies go out of business fast. If you want to do this work, look for a company that has been around a long time.

Bodyguards guard a wealthy, famous, or threatened person. They must be strong and fit. They may need a license to carry a gun.

Gate tenders sit at gates of private homes or

businesses. They let in only the people who are on a list.

Campus police are hired by colleges. They work on the grounds of the college.

Questions to Ask Yourself

Law enforcement careers in private companies tend to require less training than in other areas. 1) What type of training does a security guard need? 2) What about a private eye?

How to Prepare for a Law-Enforcement Job

5

Answer these questions before you say for sure that a career in law enforcement is right for you. All of these are important ways to get ready for a law-enforcement job, so be honest.

Do you obey the law? That means you don't do drugs, steal, or have a bad driving record. Your teachers and other adults must see you as a person they can trust. You can still have fun, hang out with friends, join clubs, and belong to a baseball team. Just don't spend your weekends drinking beer and getting in trouble. Almost every job in law enforcement is closed to you if you get a police record after age sixteen.

Do you stay fit? For law enforcement work you must be healthy and strong.

Do you read a newspaper or a magazine at least once a week? Most law-enforcement jobs require you to read well and understand what you read.

Do you write well? Almost all of the jobs require you to write reports.

Do you know how to use a computer? Every police department will soon be using computers.

Do you take courses in school to prepare you for a law-enforcement job? Some useful courses are psychology, marriage and the family (police are often called to break up family fights), sociology, civics, law, and science.

If you think a law-enforcement career might be right for you, here are other ways to prepare yourself. In these ways, you can gain experience that will help you get a job in law enforcement.

Volunteer to help with neighborhood watch programs. Take your turn walking around the neighborhood to spot trouble spots and report them to the police.

Take courses in martial arts or other self-defense courses. Being able to defend yourself without a gun is great training for many of the jobs.

Take a course in defensive driving. Some places offer courses that do more than teach you how to drive. They teach you how to drive under bad conditions.

Attend DARE (Drug Abuse Resistance Education) meetings, ride-along programs, junior police, police club, or other programs offered by police. These give you a firsthand look at police as people.

Take first-aid, lifesaving, and CPR courses. These will prepare you to help in emergencies.

Learn a second language. Many people in the United States do not speak English. Knowing another language is a big plus in getting a job.

Volunteer for jobs in which you work with people. Lots of jobs in your school and community can give you a taste of working with people of all ages and types. Check out what you can do in a local hospital, fire station, or place of worship.

Next Step

Now that you have looked at law-enforcement jobs, you may have decided whether law enforcement seems right for you.

If you have concluded that law enforcement work is not for you, you have made a good decision. No one should go into law-enforcement work unless it is right for him or her. You will find your job, but just not in this field. Keep looking.

If you have decided that none of the jobs is *quite* right for you, but you still like the idea of police work, don't give up. Look for a job that lets you work around the police and help the police. Some of these jobs are secretary, file clerk, cleaning person, and maintenance worker. All of these jobs require you to pass only the tests for your job and to have a clean police record.

In small towns and counties you may be able to get one of these jobs by talking directly to the chief of police or sheriff. In larger cities you must apply for one of these positions through the regular municipal or county personnel office; once hired, you must request a transfer to the police or sheriff's department whenever there is an opening. The police will tell you that the people who do these jobs are real helpers. If you do your job well, you can be sure that you are doing important work for law enforcement.

If you think you have found a job that looks really right for you, good for you. Now do the rest of your homework. Call some of the places listed in the next chapter to get more information about that job. Talk to people who do that job right now, and ask them to tell you more. Then apply for the job. The next chapter will tell you how to do that.

Questions to Ask Yourself

It can be difficult to decide on a career. You may have decided that a career in law enforcement is for you. 1) If so, what courses are offered in your school or community that will help you in beginning a career in law enforcement? 2) How can you talk to someone doing the job that interests you? 3) What kinds of questions would you ask him or her about the job?

Applying for a Job in Law Enforcement

6

How to Find a Full-time Job

If you are seeking a local government job, turn to the blue pages of the telephone book. There you will find the telephone number of your municipal or county personnel office. Call and ask how to find what jobs are open and what you need to do to apply. Check also under the heading Employment Service in the list of Frequently Called Numbers at the front of your telephone book.

If a job with the state government appeals to you, look up the telephone number of your state personnel office in the blue pages of the telephone book. Also check under Job Line— Employment Service Information in the white pages. Call and ask how you can find out what jobs are open. They can also tell you what you need to do to get the jobs and the educational requirements.

If you want a federal government job, look in the blue pages for a Federal Job

Information Center. If one is not listed, dial the operator and ask for the number in your state. At that number they can tell you about job openings, what you need to do to get the jobs, and the educational requirements.

For information on becoming a postal police officer, check at your local post office. Look for a list of openings on their bulletin board.

To find out about opportunities in private businesses and industry, start at your State Personnel Office. Call them and ask about the kind of job that interests you.

Many cities and counties also give job-hunting help. Ask a high school counselor in your town to tell you if your town provides special help.

Visit some large companies in your area and ask if they are hiring guards. If they are, ask at the front desk for the personnel office. Remember to dress neatly and to speak in a polite and confident manner.

Look in the yellow pages of the telephone book under Security Guard and Patrol Services. Remember to check if the companies you are interested in are licensed.

Finding Part-time Work

Your best route to a part-time job is through an agency that hires security people and sends them out on jobs. Look in the yellow pages under Security Guard and Patrol Services. Call a few agencies and ask if they hire part-time workers.

Some cities also hire part-time crossing guards for school crossings. Look up the number of your local Police Department and ask if they hire crossing guards.

For Still More Help

If you or your school is online with a service such America Online (AOL) or is on the Internet directly, you can get information from people who are in law enforcement. You may also see job openings advertised on the Internet. Find a topic heading that interests you. Post your questions on the bulletin board in that topic. Ask people to e-mail answers to you. In AOL, for example, look under the topic "Public Safety Center." Then go to "Special Interest" topics and check out "Corrections Officers."

If you need to take an exam for the job you want, ask your librarian to help you find the Arco publications in your library. These are a

Call the personnel departments of the companies you would like to work for to find out about job openings.

series of handbooks that give you an idea of what police exams and civil service exams are like.

Job hunting is slow work. You will probably have to apply at more than one place before you get a job. Most people do. You may even need to work another job while you hunt for your job in law enforcement.

Let everyone know you are job hunting. Tell your neighbors, friends, teachers, and counselor. The more people who know you are interested, the more likely you are to hear about a job opening.

Don't be in a hurry to hear from an agency to which you have applied. Many places check out your background before they let you know if they will hire you. If you have not heard in three weeks, call and ask politely if you have been hired or not.

Don't take a job because you are in a hurry. If you really want to do law enforcement, wait for the right job. You will spend many years of your life working. Work at something you like. You owe it to yourself. And if you do find a law-enforcement job that is right for you, you will make the world a safer place.

Questions to Ask Yourself

There are several ways to find out about job listings in the field of law enforcement. 1) How would you find a job listing for the federal government? 2) How about for the position of postal police officer? 3) How can you use the Internet to help in your job search?

Glossary

Armed Services Vocational Aptitude Battery
(ASVAB) Written test given by all the armed services.

armored car Bulletproof truck made to carry money and other valuables.

automatic alarm Alarm on goods sold in stores.

beat The area that a police officer patrols.

body armor Bulletproof shirt worn by some law-enforcement officers.

bulletproof vest *See* body armor.

cadet Person in training to become a police officer.

criminal Someone who breaks a law.

CPR Cardiopulmonary resuscitation; a method of keeping a person's heart pumping and lungs breathing.

enforce To uphold; to carry out.

Federal Law Enforcement Training Center
(FLETC) School in Glynco, Georgia, where nearly all federal law-enforcement workers

who have any police power are sent to be trained.

inmate Anyone held in a jail or prison.

interstate roads Main highways that crisscross the United States.

license Certification provided by the state for a person to undertake an activity.

limited police power Authority for a law-enforcement officer to enforce only certain laws.

minimum wage Standard amount of pay set by the federal government.

monitor Screen of a television or a computer that shows the picture.

offender Someone that the police suspect has broken a law, or someone who is arrested for a crime.

oral test A test in which you say, not write, the answers to questions.

personnel office Employment office.

physical or physical exam Test done by a doctor or nurse to find out how healthy and fit you are.

probation Period of time after a person is released from prison when his behavior and actions are carefully watched by law-enforcement officials.

rank Position or class.

shift or shift work   The twenty-four-hour day is divided into three eight-hour work units or two twelve-hour units called shifts.

shoplifter   Anyone who takes anything from a store without paying for it.

sixth sense   Instinct.

stake out   When police officers watch a place in anticipation of a crime or the arrival of a person suspected of a crime.

written test   Test in which you write the answers to questions.

For Further Reading

Akin, Richard H. *The Private Investigator's Basic Manual*. Springfield, IL: C.C. Thomas, 1976.

Career Opportunities in the National Park Service. Washington, DC: Dept. of the Interior, National Park Service, 1978.

Cohen, Paul, and Cohen, Shari. *Careers in Law Enforcement and Security*. New York: Rosen Publishing Group, 1995.

Cuomo, George. *A Couple of Cops: On the Street, In the Crime Lab*. New York: Random House, 1995.

Gartner, Bob. *Careers in the National Parks, rev. ed*. New York: Rosen Publishing Group, 1996.

Mahoney, Thomas, *Law Enforcement Careers Planning*. Springfield, IL: C.C. Thomas, 1989.

For More Information

For lists of all city and state police departments, call:

Knight Line USA, (800) 738-4823.
There is a fee for the lists.

Or call or write to the agency below that handles the job you are interested in. Ask for the name and phone number of someone in your area to request information on job openings.

American Correctional Association (ACA)
8025 Laurel Lakes Court
Laurel, MD 20707-5075
(301) 918-1800

American Federation of Government
   Employees
80 F Street NW
Washington, DC 20001
(202) 737-8700

American Federation of State, County and
  Municipal Employees
1625 L Street, NW
Washington , DC. 20036
(202) 429-1000

International Association of Chiefs of Police
515 North Washington Street
Alexandria, VA 22314
(703) 243-6500

National Federation of Federal Employees
1016 Sixteenth Street NW
Washington, DC 20036
(202) 737-8700

United States Coast Guard
(410) 768-5454

United States Army, Navy or Marines
Check at local recruiting office.

Index

About the Author
Claudine Gibson Wirths, M.A., M.Ed, has held many positions, including adjunct professor, coordinator of a career placement program for students with severe learning disabilities, and elementary school science teacher. Ms. Wirths has also served as a research consultant to many public and private agencies, including ten years with the Aiken, South Carolina, Police Department. She has co-authored thirteen books, and several articles and monographs.

Photo Credits: Cover © Michael Lichter/International Stock; p. 2 © Earl Dotter/Impact Visuals; p. 8 © Clark Jones/Impact Visuals; p. 12 © F. M. Kearney/Impact Visuals; p. 17 © R. Tesa/ International Stock; p. 18 © Bill Stanton/International Stock; p. 25 © Phyllis Picardi/International Stock; p. 27 © AP/Wide World Photos; p. 30 © Stefan Lawrence/International Stock; p. 35 Martha Tabor/Impact Visuals; p. 37 © Scott Thode/International Stock; p. 42 © Miriam Romais/Impact Visuals; p. 45 © Ryan Williams/ International Stock; p. 55 by Kim Sonsky.

Design: Erin McKenna